SCIENTIFIC AMERICAN. EDUCATIONAL PUBLISHING

SOLID START

10 FUN

EXPERIMENTS WITH THE STATES OF MATTER

T0054133

BRING SCIENCE HOME

Published in 2024 by The Rosen Publishing Group, Inc.
2544 Clinton Street, Buffalo, NY 14224

Contains material from Scientific American , a division of Springer Nature America, Inc., reprinted by permission as well as original material from The Rosen Publishing Group.

Copyright © 2024 by The Rosen Publishing Group, Inc.

First Edition

All rights reserved. No part of this book may be reproduced in any form without permission in writing from the publisher, except by a reviewer.

Editor: Kristen Rajczak Nelson
Designer: Rachel Rising

Activity on p. 5 by Science Buddies(July 24, 2014); p. 9 by Science Buddies, Sabine De Brabandere (March 7, 2019); p. 15 by Science Buddies, Sabine De Brabandere (June 8, 2017); p. 21 by Science Buddies (August 27, 2015); p. 27 Science Buddies (October 31, 2013); p. 33 Science Buddies (May 26, 2016); p. 41 Science Buddies, Megan Arnett (June 29, 2017); p. 46 Science Buddies (June 5, 2014); p. 52 Science Buddies, Svenja Lohner (October 12, 2017); p. 57 Science Buddies, Svenja Lohner (September 14, 2017).

All illustrations by Continuum Content Solutions

Photo Credits: pp. 3, 4, 21, 24, 27, 30, 46, 50, 52, 55 cve iv/Shutterstock.com; pp. 5, 9, 15, 21, 27, 33, 41, 46, 52, 57 Anna Frajtova/Shutterstock.com.

Names: Scientific American, Inc.
Title: Solid start: 10 fun experiments with the states of matter / edited by the Scientific American Editors.
Description: New York : Scientific American Educational Publishing, 2024. | Series: Bring science home | Includes glossary and index.
Identifiers: ISBN 9781725349247 (pbk.) | ISBN 9781725349254 (library bound) | ISBN 9781725349261 (ebook)
Subjects: LCSH: Matter--Properties--Experiments--Juvenile literature. | Science--Experiments--Juvenile literature. | Science projects--Juvenile literature.
Classification: LCC QC173.36 S65 2024 | DDC 530.4078--dc23

Manufactured in the United States of America

Some of the images in this book illustrate individuals who are models. The depictions do not imply actual situations or events.

CPSIA Compliance Information: Batch #CSSA24. For further information contact Rosen Publishing, New York, New York at 1-800-237-9932.

Find us on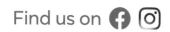

CONTENTS

 THESE ACTIVITIES INCLUDE
SCIENCE FAIR PROJECT IDEAS.

INTRODUCTION

Solids, liquids, and gases are all states of matter that have characteristics that can be easily observed. In the following experiments, you will learn more about how liquids—and sometimes solids!—flow, that gases have density, the structure of solids, and much more. Use materials from around your home to explore the states of matter!

Projects marked with ⚛ include a section called Science Fair Project Ideas. These ideas can help you develop your own original science fair project. Science fair judges tend to reward creative thought and imagination, and it helps if you are really interested in your project. You will also need to follow the scientific method. See page 61 for more information about that.

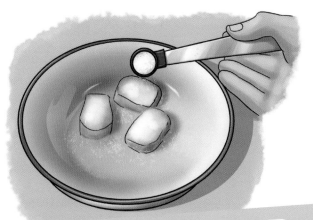

What Makes Ice Melt Fastest?

GET READY TO FREEZE AND MELT WITH THIS CHEMISTRY CHALLENGE!

Do you sometimes dump ice cubes into a drink to help keep cool on a hot summer day? Have you ever watched the ice cubes melt and wondered how you could make them melt more slowly—or even faster? In this science activity, you will get to try some different, common household substances to try and answer this question: What will help a solid ice cube turn into a liquid puddle the fastest?

PROJECT TIME
30 minutes

KEY CONCEPTS
Water
Ice
Chemistry
Solutions
Phases of matter

5

BACKGROUND ·····························

Temperature isn't the only thing that affects how a liquid freezes—and melts. If you've ever made homemade ice cream the old-fashioned way using a hand-crank machine, you probably know that you need ice and salt to freeze the cream mixture. Similarly, if you live in a cold climate, you've probably seen the trucks that salt and sand the streets after a snowfall to prevent ice from building up on the roads. In both of these instances, salt is lowering the freezing point of water, which means that the water needs to be colder to turn from liquid into ice. For the ice cream maker, the temperature of the ice-salt mixture can get much lower than if just using normal ice, and this makes it possible to freeze the ice cream mixture. For the salt spread on streets, lowering the freezing point means that ice can melt even when the outdoor temperature is below water's freezing point. Both of these events demonstrate "freezing point depression."

Salt mixed with water is an example of a chemical solution. In a solution, there is a solute (salt in this example) that gets dissolved in a solvent (water in this case). When other substances are mixed with water, they may also lower its freezing point. In this science activity, you'll investigate how salt, sand, and sugar affect water's freezing point.

MATERIALS ~~~~~~~~~~~~~~~~~~

- Four ice cubes (They should all be the same size and shape.)
- Four drinking glasses (They should all be identical.)
- Table salt
- Sugar
- Sand
- 1/4 teaspoon measuring spoon

PREPARATION ·····················

- Prepare (or purchase) some ice cubes if you do not have any ready. They should all be the same size and shape.

PROCEDURE

- Into each drinking glass, place one ice cube. Make sure the ice cube is oriented the same way in each glass. (**Tip**: If you are using ice cubes from a tray, it helps to let the tray sit at room temperature for about five minutes so that the ice cubes more easily come out of the tray cups and do not break into pieces.)

- Carefully sprinkle 1/4 teaspoon of salt over the ice cube in one drinking glass. Then sprinkle 1/4 teaspoon of sugar over the cube in another glass and 1/4 teaspoon of sand over the ice in the third. Do not sprinkle anything over the ice cube in the fourth glass. (It will be your control.) *How do you think the salt, sugar, and sand will affect how quickly the ice cubes melt?*

- Set the drinking glasses aside somewhere indoors, out of direct sunlight.

- Watch the ice cubes over time, checking on them every five to 10 minutes. *After around 30 minutes, which cube has melted the most? Which is the first one to melt completely? Which is the last?*

- *Overall, how do you think added salt, sugar, or sand affects how quickly the ice melts? Can you explain why this might be?*

ExTRA

You could try this activity at different temperatures, such as in the refrigerator or outside on a hot day. *How does adding salt, sugar, or sand to the cubes affect how quickly they melt when exposed to a hotter or colder environment?*

ExTRA

In this activity, you used 1/4 teaspoon of each substance, but you could try adding more or less. *Does the melting rate depend on the amount of the substance added?*

7

ExTRA

Identify some other substances to test on the ice cubes. Do other substances help melt the cubes more quickly or do they end up melting more slowly?

OBSERVATIONS AND RESULTS

Did the ice cube sprinkled with table salt melt the fastest?

In this activity, you tried adding salt, sugar, or sand to ice to see whether the substance would help melt the ice. In other words, you wanted to test whether these substances could demonstrate freezing point depression, or the lowering of the ice's freezing point so that it melted into a liquid at a lower temperature than normal. You should have seen that the ice cube with salt sprinkled on it melted faster than any of the other cubes. This is because the amount by which the freezing point is lowered depends on the number of molecules dissolved, but not their chemical nature. (This is an example of what's called a "colligative property.") In the same volume, there are more molecules of salt than there are of sugar or sand because the chemical components that make up the salt are much smaller than the sugar or sand.

CLEANUP

You can dump the salt and water mixture and sugar and water mixture into the sink. Be sure not to pour the sand down a sink drain or garbage disposal! Instead, throw out the damp sand outside or in a trash can. Return all materials to where you found them.

Salt on Ice

WHY DOES ICE GET WEIRD WHEN SALT IS ADDED?
USE A LITTLE KITCHEN CHEMISTRY TO FIND OUT!

Have you ever wondered why ice cubes in your cold drink become gradually smaller or why their surface becomes smoother as they melt? Does ice always melt this way? In this activity, you will use water balloons to create giant ice balls and observe how they melt. Can you predict the effect a bit of salt will have on your giant ice ball?

PROJECT TIME

 20 minutes, plus overnight preparation

KEY CONCEPTS

Chemistry
Temperature
Solid
Liquid
Freezing point

9

BACKGROUND ••

All matter is made up of tiny particles, and temperature is a measure of how much these tiny particles move. Even the particles in a solid like ice move—they vibrate. But because they are cold, they do not wiggle much and can hold onto one another. In the case of water, the particles arrange themselves in a regular lattice.

When ice is surrounded by air or liquid, at room temperature it absorbs heat from its surroundings. As a result, the tiny particles in the ice start to vibrate more. Those at the edge might break loose and flow freely over and alongside one another and the ice. At this stage, water and ice coexist. This is an active process—some particles break loose whereas others attach to the solid. Because the surroundings are at a higher temperature, more break loose than reattach so we see the ice melt. For pure water this coexistence of water and ice happens at 32°F (0°C). When the surroundings are cooler, heat will flow to the surroundings, cooling down the water particles. As a result, more particles attach to the lattice, and we see the ice grow.

When table salt (sodium chloride) is dissolved in water, its sodium and chloride atoms are added to the water particles. These make it more difficult for water particles to arrange themselves in a regular lattice and solidify into ice. That is why you need to cool salt water well below 32°F (0°C) before it becomes ice.

When pure ice is surrounded by a saltwater solution at room temperature, particles at the edge of the ice will absorb heat, break loose, and flow freely. At the same time, some water particles might try to reattach. Will the sodium and chlorine particles be in the way, making it more difficult for the water particles to reattach to the ice and causing the ice to melt faster? Do this activity to find out!

MATERIALS ~~~~~~~~~~~~~~~

- At least two water balloons
- Water
- Freezer
- Oven mitt
- Small plates
- Cup
- Table salt
- Water dropper, baster or syringe
- Food coloring, preferably liquid
- Work space that can get wet
- Towel to wipe your work space

PREPARATION

- The day before you plan to do the activity, fill a balloon with water, tie it with a knot and freeze it overnight. Freeze at least two balloons for each person doing the activity.

- Just before you plan to start the activity, fill a cup with water and add food coloring.

- Choose an area that can get wet to do the activity.

PROCEDURE

- Put on oven mitts and retrieve the two frozen water balloons from the freezer.

- Peel off the balloon skin so you are left with two ice balls. (Some ice balls might be in a pear shape rather than a ball—that is fine.)

- Place each ice ball on a small plate and place them next to each other. *What do you think will happen if you sprinkle salt on the ice ball?*

- Sprinkle about 1/8 teaspoon of salt on the top of each ice ball, add a few drops of colored water to moisten the salt, and observe.

- Wait a few minutes. *What happens? Is it what you predicted?*

- Drip more colored water over the top of the ice ball on the left. Leave the other untouched. *Do you think one ball will melt faster than the other? If so, which one and why?*

- Observe, and intermittently drip water over the left ball, leaving the other untouched. Use your dropper, baster, or syringe to suck up the water collected in the plate and drip it back over the left ice ball. You may need to discard water from the plate when it looks like it may overflow. *Does one ball melt faster than the other does? Why do you think this is the case?*

- Occasionally sprinkle more salt on top of both ice balls, followed by a few drops of colored water to wet the salt. *What happens when you add more salt?*

- *Can you see patterns appear in the ice? If so, are the patterns on the two ice balls similar? Can you explain what you observe?*

ExTRA
Have fun adding food coloring, salt, and water. *Can you make beautiful patterns?*

ExTRA
Hold a flashlight behind your melting ice balls and see how the patterns light up.

ExTRA
Explore other scenarios, such as sprinkling salt without adding a few drops of water or dripping saltwater over the ice balls. *Do these changes impact the ice differently? Why do you think would this be the case?*

OBSERVATIONS AND RESULTS ··········

Did you see how the ice melts faster where it is in contact with wet salt? Did streams of melted water appear on the left ice ball, and did deep caverns pierce through the ice on the other ball?

When ice melts, water and ice coexist. Because salt particles make it harder for water particles to freeze back onto the ice, the ice that is in contact with dissolved salt melts faster. When the saltwater flows over the surface, it melts the ice on its way, creating channels, like rivers, over the surface of the ice ball.

When the saltwater is trapped in one location, such as in the case of the ice ball on the right, it erodes a path down into the ice, creating sharp ridges or peaks. Food coloring makes these patterns more visible.

When salt is sprinkled over the ice without adding water, the salt will dissolve in meltwater and have the same effect—it only takes a little longer to see the results.

CLEANUP ·

Pour your melted ice balls in to the sink. Wash and dry the plates you used. Put away all materials you used.

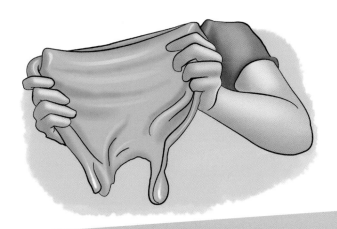

Slime
Is It a Solid, Liquid—or Both?

STRETCH IT, SMOOSH IT, LEAVE IT—WHAT IS IT? TRY YOUR HAND AT SOME POLYMER CHEMISTRY TO FIND OUT MORE ABOUT THE STRANGE NATURE OF SLIME!

PROJECT TIME

45 minutes

KEY CONCEPTS

Solid
Fluid
Viscosity
Non-Newtonian fluid

A rabbit is fluffy, mud is squishy, and a balloon is stretchy. What substances can be fluffy, squishy, and stretchy at the same time, and are so much fun to play with? Silly Putty, Gak, and slime! These substances can be confusing too. Most substances become harder when cooled and flow much better as they warm up. Think of how honey slowly oozes from the bottle on a cold day and rushes out on a hot day. Silly Putty, Gak, and slime are different. They can feel as hard as a solid when squeezed in your fist, but as soon as you release your grip, they ooze out through your fingers like a thick liquid. Why would slime be different? In this activity, you will make your own slime, play with it and discover what makes it flow!

15

BACKGROUND ••••••••••••••••••••••••••••••••

Is it a solid or a liquid? Solids consist of tightly packed particles called molecules or atoms that clasp onto each other so the solid holds its shape. Liquids have particles that can slide over and around one another, allowing the fluid to flow. Only adding or taking away heat can make some liquids, like water or oil, flow better or worse. These are called Newtonian liquids. Non-Newtonian liquids, such as ketchup and slime, are different. Manipulations like squeezing, stirring, or agitating can also change how they flow. Sometimes they can become so viscous—or have such a hard time flowing—that they could easily be mistaken for a solid.

One such non-Newtonian liquid can be created with white school glue, which is a polymer. A polymer is made from long chains of repeating parts called monomers. One polymer might consist of hundreds of thousands of monomers. Polymers are also called macromolecules, or large-sized molecules. Some are human-made, such as plastic and nylon. Others occur in nature, such as DNA, wheat gluten, and starches.

White school glue is liquid because its long polymers can slide over and along one another. It does not flow easily, though; it is quite viscous. The addition of some chemicals—such as a borax solution (or sodium tetraborate decahydrate dissolved in water)—can cause cross-links to form between the polymers. It is as if the very long molecules started to hold hands. Will the result still be a fluid where the polymers can glide over each other, or will it become a solid?

MATERIALS ~~~~~~~~~~~~~~~~

- Container
- White school glue or other polyvinyl acetate (PVA) glue
- Hot water
- Stirring rod or plastic spoon
- Borax
- Measuring spoon (1/2 tablespoon)
- Measuring cups (1/2 and 1/4 cups)
- Goggles or eye protection (handling borax can irritate eyes)
- A work space (and work clothing) that is protected and won't be damaged if sticky slime gets on it

- Adult helper
- Food coloring or marker (optional)
- Ziplock bag or airtight container to store your slime (optional)

PREPARATION

- Protect your work space and clothing—slime can be sticky and hard to remove!

- Put on goggles or glasses, as the borax solution can irritate the eyes.

- Have an adult helper stir 1/2 tablespoon of borax powder into 1/2 cup (118 ml) of lukewarm water in a cup. Stir well until the solution looks clear, label the container "2 percent borax solution," and set aside.

PROCEDURE

- Pour 1/2 cup (118 ml) of glue and 1/4 cup (59 ml) of warm water in a container. Note that this solution is 2/3 (or 67 percent) glue.

- Optional: If you like colored slime, you can mix in a few drops of food coloring. Another option is to put the tip of a marker into the water for a short time, so the ink dissolves in the water.

- Stir the glue/water mixture with the stirring rod.

- Add 5 tablespoons (74 ml) of the borax solution to your glue/water mix.

- Stir with the stirring rod. After some stirring, you should see a substance sticking to your stirrer. *Does the sticky substance look like a solid or like a liquid—or can you not tell yet?*

17

- If your substance is still watery, add more borax solution 1/4 tablespoon (4 ml) at a time until there is very little watery solution left.

- Collect the sticky substance in your hands and work it with your hands for about one minute. *How does the slime feel? How does the stickiness and stretchiness change when you work it for a while?*

- *Would you say the slime is a liquid, or is it more like a solid?*

- Squeeze your slime into an oval and use both hands to pull it apart quickly. *Does it tear or elongate?*

- Squeeze your slime into an oval again and use both hands to pull it apart slowly. *Does it tear or elongate? How thin can you get it?*

- Work your slime with your hands to form a ball. Try to stick your finger into it forcefully. *How deep does your finger go? Does it feel like you poked your finger into something solid, or something liquid?*

- Now try to stick your finger into it gently. *How deep does your finger go? Does it feel like you poked your finger into something solid or something liquid?*

- Squeeze your slime into a ball again and put it in a container. *What do you think will happen if you leave it there for a while? Will it stay in an oval, like a solid would do, or will it relax into a puddle and take the form of the container, like a liquid would do?*

- Optional: To keep your slime nice and soft, store it in an airtight container or ziptop bag.

ExTRA

Add other substances, such as shaving cream or liquid soap, to your glue/water solution. *Will you still obtain slime? How will this slime feel and look different?*

ExTRA

Leave your slime uncovered for a day. *What do you think will happen? Will it become more like a solid, or start to flow easier? Why do you think this will happen?*

OBSERVATIONS AND RESULTS

Did the slime sometimes feel like a solid and sometimes like a fluid? This is expected.

This type of slime thickens or becomes harder or more viscous when you squeeze or stir it. This happens because it is made up of very long particles that are cross-linked. When you leave the particles alone they will coil up, and the coils can slide over each other. When you apply pressure by squeezing or stirring, some coils unwind and become entangled, making it harder for the slime to flow.

When you stirred your slime, tried to rip it apart or poked your finger into it with force, the polymers were entangled and it looked like a solid. As a result, it was hard to stir, it ripped apart, and your finger bounced back.

When you left your slime alone to rest, gently pulled it apart, or gently poked your finger in it, the polymers were curled up. They could slide over one another, and it felt more like a liquid. As a result, the slime took the form of the container, it could be stretched thin, and your finger could move through it. It did not flow as easily as water because it consists of long cross-linked particles, whereas water consists of small particles. When a substance keeps its volume but loses its form when left alone, scientists call it a liquid.

CLEANUP

Do not pour glue solutions or slime down a drain because they can form clogs. Instead, throw them away in the garbage. Wash all equipment with soapy water.

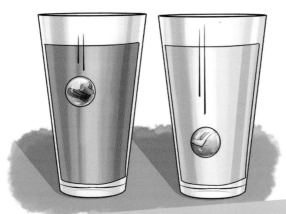

Marble Race in Liquid!

SYRUP OR HONEY? OIL OR WATER? WHO WILL WIN IN THIS LIQUID, MARBLE-RACE CHALLENGE? TEST THE VISCOSITY OF COMMON LIQUIDS AROUND YOUR HOUSE, AND FIND OUT!

Have you ever tried to squeeze honey or syrup out of a bottle at breakfast on a chilly winter morning? Do you notice that it's harder to do that than on a hot summer day? As the liquid gets colder, its viscosity, or resistance to flow, increases. Viscosity is a property of liquids that can be very important in very different applications—from how the syrup flows out of your bottle to how blood flows through the human body to how lava flows out of a volcano. In this project, you will learn a little bit about viscosity by holding a marble race!

PROJECT TIME

30 minutes

KEY CONCEPTS

Physics
Friction
Solids
Liquids

BACKGROUND

You experience friction all around you. It is what allows your shoes to grip the floor so you don't slip, and it's what makes your bike come to a stop when you squeeze the brakes. This type of friction is a force that resists motion between two solid objects. Liquids, however, have friction, too—not just against solids (for example, water against a drinking glass)—but also internal friction, the liquid against itself. This internal friction is called viscosity. Different liquids have different viscosities, which means some liquids flow more easily than others. You will notice this if you think about squirting water out of a bottle or squirt gun. Imagine how much harder that would be to do with cold syrup!

There are several different ways scientists can measure the viscosity of a liquid. One method is called a "falling sphere viscometer," in which you drop a sphere (such as a marble) through a tube filled with liquid. By measuring how long it takes the marble to fall and how far it travels, you can figure out the liquid's viscosity. You won't need to do any calculations in this activity—but you will get to "race" marbles by dropping them in different liquids. Will viscosity affect how fast the marbles fall? Try this project to find out!

MATERIALS

- About a dozen equal-size marbles
- At least two equal-size tall, transparent drinking glasses (the taller the better)
- Liquids from around your kitchen you have permission to use, such as water, syrup, honey, molasses, olive oil, vegetable oil, etcetera
- Strainer or colander

- A flat surface that can have liquids (water, oil, etcetera) spilled on it—or protection (such as a large trash bag) for the surface
- Optional: Extra bowls/containers and/or a funnel (for storing and reusing the liquids you use for the activity, if you do not want to throw them away)
- Optional: Volunteer to help you see which marble hits the bottom first

PREPARATION

- If you want to save and reuse the liquids you use from the activity, make sure you thoroughly wash your marbles and drinking glasses with soap and water, then dry them completely. This will ensure they are clean and you do not get your liquids dirty.

- Prepare a work space on your flat surface and ensure that it is ready for any accidental spills (of water, oil, etcetera).

PROCEDURE

- Fill your two (or more) drinking glasses with each of your different liquids to the same height. (To avoid spilling when you drop the marbles in, do not fill them all the way to the brim.)

- *Which liquid do you think has a higher viscosity? Can you tell when you pour them into the glasses? Do you think the marble will fall faster through one of the liquids?*

- Hold one marble in each hand, just above the surface of the liquid in each glass.

- Watch the glasses closely. Be prepared to watch the bottom to see which marble hits first. If you have a volunteer, have them look at the glasses too.

- Let the marbles go at exactly the same time.

- Observe which marble hits the bottom of the glass first.

- *Which marble won the "race"? Do your results match your prediction?*

- Repeat the activity with a few more marbles to see if you get the same results. (Use clean, dry marbles each time.)

23

- If you have more than two different liquids, you can try racing marbles in other liquids to see what happens.

- *Through which liquid do the marbles fall the fastest? The slowest?*

ExTRA

What happens if you drop different types of marbles (for example, steel marbles versus glass marbles) or different size marbles? Do the results of your races change?

⚛ SCIENCE FAIR IDEA

What happens if you change the temperature of a liquid? Have an adult help you cool some syrup in the refrigerator and heat some on the stove or in the microwave. *What happens if you do a race with cold versus warm syrup instead of room-temperature syrup? How does temperature affect the liquid's viscosity? Is the temperature effect stronger on some liquids than it is for others?*

OBSERVATIONS AND RESULTS · · · · · · · · ·

When pouring your liquids, you might have noticed that some of them were "thicker" or harder to pour. These are the more viscous liquids. You can also think about what these liquids are like when you use them every day. For example, what would happen if you poured water on pancakes? Would it flow slowly like syrup or spread out very quickly? What about if you tried to pour and drink a glass of syrup? Would that be harder than drinking a glass of water?

You should have observed that the marbles fell more slowly through more viscous liquids (such as syrup) than through less viscous liquids (such as water). This is because the more viscous liquids have more resistance to flow, making it more difficult for the marble to travel through them. It might be hard to tell the difference between the results for some liquids, however—especially if your glasses are not very tall. This is why it is important to do multiple trials and have a volunteer help watch the marbles.

CLEANUP

If you want to keep the remaining liquids for future use, have an adult help you pour them back into storage containers. (Use the strainer to remove the marbles). Otherwise, have an adult help you dispose of the liquids properly. Be careful because pouring some viscous liquids (such as cooking oil) down the sink can clog the drain.

⚛ Spilling Science
Can Solid Candies Flow Like Liquids?

EXPLORE STATES OF MATTER IN
THIS TASTY PHYSICS PROJECT.

PROJECT TIME

 30 minutes

KEY CONCEPTS

Physics
Liquids
Solids
Size
Density

Have you ever poured sand out of a bucket or cereal out of a box and noticed it seems to flow a lot like water? This is because both sand and cereal are granular materials. That means they're made up of solid particles, but they can actually flow like liquids! Candies such as Skittles, M&Ms, Nerds, and many others are also granular materials. In this science activity, you'll investigate how the size and shape of granular materials affect how they flow. And what better way to do this investigation than with some sweets! So get ready to put your Halloween candy to some good scientific use.

BACKGROUND ....

Solid matter (such as sand) that is made up of many individual small particles is called a granular material, and the individual particles are called grains. Granular materials can range in size from small powders such as sugar and flour to large objects such as rocks and boulders. Note that the word "grain" doesn't just refer to things you'd traditionally call grains, such as sand or rice; it can be any object or particle in a granular material.

For a granular material to behave like a liquid, there must be many, many grains close together. For example, a single boulder rolling down a hill is not acting like a liquid; but thousands of rocks, boulders, and dirt particles flowing down a hill during a landslide *do* behave like a liquid. When granular materials flow like a liquid, it's called granular flow. Understanding granular flow is important for many industries that put things like candy, cereal, or pills into bottles or bags. In these factories, granular materials usually flow out of a large container called a hopper and through a funnel. To put the right amount in each bottle or bag engineers need to know the granular flow rate of the materials through the funnel.

MATERIALS ～～～～～～～

- Clear plastic water bottle, about 1 pint (560 ml)
- Scissors
- Ruler
- Measuring cup (a graduated one with a spout works best)
- Adult helper
- Bowl, medium to large in size
- At least three types of candies with different sizes, such as Nerds, Junior Mints, and M&Ms. You'll want at least 1 cup of each type.

(Alternatively, you could use other types of small, solid materials. Tip: For the best results, try to only use candies with similar surface textures and avoid very lightweight candies such as ones that are hollow or air-puffed).

- Sheet of paper and pen or pencil
- Stopwatch
- Calculator

PREPARATION

· Have an adult prepare the bottle so it can be used as a funnel. To do this, carefully cut the bottom off (as close to the end as possible) and carefully cut the top off until the opening size is about 1.3 inches (3.3 cm) in diameter.

PROCEDURE

· Measure out at least 1 cup of the largest type of candy you want to test. The more candy you use, the better your results will be. *Exactly how many cups of candy did you measure out?* Write this down on a piece of paper.

· Take the bottle you cut and flip it upside down. Have a helper hold the funnel over a bowl and plug the opening (which should now be at the bottom) with their hand. Pour the measured candy into the top and make sure none leaks out the bottom.

· Get the stopwatch ready, and then have the helper quickly remove their hand and gently shake the funnel. Time how long it takes all of the material to go through the funnel and into the bowl below. *How long did it take for all of the candy to leave the funnel?* Write this down on your piece of paper. **Tip:** If the material jams the funnel, have an adult make the opening a little larger and try this again. Also be sure the helper is gently shaking the funnel during the entire time the candy is flowing.

· Calculate the volumetric flow rate of the candy. To do this, divide the volume of the candy by the time it took to finish flowing through the funnel. For example, if you used 1 cup of M&Ms and it took two seconds to flow through, the volumetric flow rate would be 1/2 cup per second. *What is the volumetric flow rate of your candy?*

· You may want to try this process a few more times with the same type of candy to see how accurate your results are. Each time you test the candy be sure to hold the funnel from about the same height above the bowl and shake the funnel in the same way.

- Try this entire process with two other types of candy that are different sizes. *What are their volumetric flow rates?*

- *Overall, do you see a correlation between the volumetric flow rate and the size of the candies you tested? Do you think other factors, such as surface texture and shape, might affect the volumetric flow rate?*

⚛ SCIENCE FAIR IDEA

In this activity, you looked at how size affects volumetric flow rate, but other factors affect the rate as well. To investigate this, try testing materials that are the same size but have a different surface texture (such as smooth versus rough or bumpy candies) or are different shapes, such as conical Candy Corns and spherical malt balls. *How do other factors affect a material's volumetric flow rate?*

⚛ SCIENCE FAIR IDEA

You could do this activity again but rather than measuring volumetric flow rate, you could measure the mass flow rate. What you would need to do is weigh your samples on a scale (or calculate their weight based on the packaging) instead of measuring them in a measuring cup. *How does the volumetric flow rate compare with the mass flow rate?*

EXTRA

You could investigate the bulk density of each material. The bulk density of a granular material is its mass per total volume that it occupies (including air space). *Does packing density correlate with the volumetric (or mass) flow rate of the materials?*

OBSERVATIONS AND RESULTS

Overall, did the smaller candies have a faster volumetric flow rate than the larger candies?

Because granular flow rate is complex, it is difficult to accurately calculate; it is affected by a number of factors, including the grains' surface texture, density both as a group and individually, and shape and size, along with the funnel opening size. To try to only investigate the effect of grain size on the granular flow rate of different granular materials you should have only used candies with similar surface textures and avoided very lightweight ones (for example, hollow or air-puffed). Under these conditions, you should have found that the smaller candies, such as Nerds, generally had a greater volumetric flow rate than the larger ones, such as Junior Mints. If you also investigated the bulk density of the candies you tested (which is measured in mass per total volume occupied, including air), you may have also seen that there is generally a positive correlation between bulk density and the flow rate. (In other words, the greater a material's bulk density, the greater its flow rate).

CLEANUP ·

Recycle the bottle used in the project. Put away the candy, or enjoy some as a snack. Be sure to share with any helpers you had! Replace all other materials where you found them.

Stacking Liquids

YOU CAN STACK BOOKS AND STACK BLOCKS, BUT DID YOU KNOW YOU CAN ALSO STACK LIQUIDS? SEE IF YOU CAN BUILD YOUR OWN LIQUID RAINBOW—IN A SINGLE CUP!

PROJECT TIME

40 minutes

KEY CONCEPTS

Physics
Chemistry
Density
Liquids

You probably know that when solid objects are placed in liquid, they can sink or float. But did you know that liquids can also sink or float? In fact, it is possible to stack different layers of liquids on top of one another. The key is that all the different layers must have different densities. You can stack them by picking several liquids with a range of densities or by varying the density of one liquid by adding chemicals such as sugar or salt to it. If you choose colored liquids or add food coloring to each layer, you can even create a whole rainbow of colors in one single glass! Want to see for yourself? In this science activity, you will stack several liquids—one by one—and create a colorful density column!

33

BACKGROUND ·······················

Whether an object sinks or floats depends on its density compared with the density of the liquid into which it is dropped. All types of matter—solids as well as liquids—are made up of many different atoms. Depending on the mass of these atoms, their size and the way they are arranged, different substances will have different densities. The density is characteristic for each individual compound and defined as the mass of a compound divided by its volume. In other words, the more matter there is in a certain amount of volume, the denser a substance is. One cubic inch (16 cu cm) of rock, for example, is much heavier than 1 cubic inch (16 cu cm)of wood. This is because there is much more matter in the same volume of rock compared with the wood.

Liquids can also have different densities. Fresh water, for example, has a density of about 1 gram per cubic centimeter at room temperature. Any compound—liquid or solid—that has a higher density than water will sink whereas substances with a lower density than that will float. You can test that for yourself by gathering several liquids that you have in your home such as vegetable oil, corn syrup, dishwashing soap, water, rubbing alcohol, and more. Which one of these do you think will sink or float in water? Find out in this activity!

MATERIALS

- Glass or cup
- Water
- Food coloring
- Scissors
- Rubber band (wide)
- Small piece of wax
- Popsicle stick
- At least two small, clear jars or transparent mini cups (2 ounces) with lids
- Permanent marker
- Masking tape
- Three tablespoons
- Dark corn syrup
- Vegetable oil
- Penny
- Paper towels
- Rubbing alcohol, dishwashing soap, and other liquids (optional)
- Sugar (optional)

PREPARATION

- Gather all your materials at a work space that can tolerate spills of all the liquids.

- Fill a cup with tap water and add a couple of drops of food coloring to the water.

- Ask an adult to help you cut and prepare small pieces (about 0.2-by-0.2 inch [0.5 by 0.5 cm]) of the rubber band, the popsicle stick, and the wax.

- Place the two empty jars in front of you (without the lids) and label them "1" and "2" with a piece of tape and the permanent marker.

PROCEDURE

- Take a clean tablespoon and pour two tablespoons full of corn syrup in jar 1.

- With the second tablespoon, carefully pour two tablespoons full of colored water into jar 1 on top of the corn syrup. *What happens to the water on top of the corn syrup? Does it mix or stay separate?*

- Use the third clean tablespoon to pour two tablespoons full of vegetable oil in jar "1" on top of the colored water. *Do you see mixing of the liquids? What happens to the oil? Does it float on top or sink to the bottom?*

- Now take empty jar 2 and add the same liquids—but in reverse order. Start by pouring in two tablespoons full of vegetable oil.

- Next, add two tablespoons full of colored water on top. *What happens to the water this time? Does it stay on top or sink to the bottom?*

- With a fresh tablespoon, carefully pour two tablespoons full of corn syrup into jar 2, on top of the water. *Does the corn syrup float on top of the other liquids? Where does it settle compared with the water and oil?*

- Wait one or two minutes to let all the liquids settle in jars 1 and 2. Then look at both jars and compare how the different liquids are layered. *Is there a difference between jar 1 and 2? Did you expect this result? Why do you think the layers turned out this way?*

- Now take jar 1 and close it with a lid. Carefully turn it upside down and set it on the table again. Observe the different liquids. *What is happening to each of the liquids? How are they layered once the jar is upside down? Did you know this would happen?*

- Compare the upside-down jar 1 with jar 2 after a couple of minutes. *Do you see any differences in layering now? What happened to each of the liquids?*

- Get all your cut-up objects and your penny ready, then drop the penny into jar 2. *What happens to the penny?*

- Next, take the piece of rubber band and drop it into jar 2. With the popsicle stick, push the rubber band all the way to the bottom of the jar. Make sure it does not stick to the bottom and can float freely. Then let go. *Where does the rubber band settle? Does it float on top, in the middle, or sit on the bottom?*

- Now drop the piece of wax into jar 2. Again, push the wax all the way down into the jar but make sure it does not stick to the jar's bottom or sides. It should be able to float freely. *What happens to the wax piece? Where does it settle compared with the rubber band?*

- Last, take the piece of popsicle stick and drop it into jar 2. Submerge it with a spoon or popsicle stick and wait for it to settle in one of the layers. *On top of which layer does the popsicle stick piece float?*

- Look at all four objects that you dropped into jar 2 and compare their locations. *Did they all settle in the same or in different liquid layers? If they are in different layers, why do you think this is the case?*

- Finally, take jar 1, which is still upside down, and shake it really hard. Then put it back on the table (this time, right side up). Observe what happens for about five to 10 minutes. *Did any of the layers mix while you shook the jar? How does the layering look after five to 10 minutes?*

ExTRA

With three liquids (vegetable oil, corn syrup, and colored water) there are six different combinations for adding the different layers on top of one another. Try all the combinations and change the order of adding the different liquids each time. *Will you always end up with the same layering result?*

ExTRA

In this activity, you had three layers of different liquids. *Can you find other household liquids that might make a fourth or fifth layer?* Some liquids to try are rubbing alcohol or dishwashing soap. *Where do you think they will settle in your density column?*

ExTRA

You can even make a density tower using the same liquid, such as water. You just have to change its density by adding different amounts of sugar to it. Try three different layers of water—each layer with the same volume of water, but one with 1 teaspoon of sugar, one with 2 teaspoons of sugar, and one with 3 teaspoons of sugar. Add different colors to each liquid to see the layers more clearly. *Which layer is on the top and which layer on the bottom? How does the amount of sugar change the density of the water? What will happen this time if you shake the jar or turn it upside down?*

ExTRA
Try to find different objects that might sink or float in the different layers of your density column. *In which layer will they settle?*

ExTRA
You can find out how much the densities of the three liquids vary by pouring the same volume of each liquid into a different cup and then weighing each of them. *How much do the masses differ? Do these results agree with your findings of how the liquids are layered?*

OBSERVATIONS AND RESULTS ··········

Did you successfully stack all three liquids on top of one another to create a colorful density column? It actually does not matter in which order you add the three different liquids into your jar; the layers will always end up being the same: The corn syrup settles on the bottom, the colored water is in the middle, and the vegetable oil floats on the top. This is because corn syrup has the highest density of all the liquids, about 1.4 grams per cubic centimeter, whereas the density of water is about 1 gram per cubic centimeter at room temperature. Vegetable oil is lighter than water with a density of about 0.9 gram per cubic centimeter and thus floats on top of the water. Even if you turn the jar upside down, the layers rearrange to the original order due to their different densities. If you did the extra activity and weighed the same volume of each liquid, you should have found that corn syrup was the heaviest, followed by water, and then the vegetable oil.

The objects that you dropped into jar 2 settled in the density column depending on their own densities. The rubber band probably settled on top of the corn syrup whereas the penny fell all the way to the bottom of the jar. The wax should have rested on top of the water layer and the popsicle stick should have floated all the way on top of the vegetable oil.

Finally, if you shook the jar really hard, you might have observed that the vegetable oil still separated and floated on top, but the corn syrup and the water layer started to mix and did not separate very easily anymore. This is due to the miscibility of the different liquids. If liquids have a very different chemical structure that makes one polar and the other one unpolar, they will not mix and always stay separate. This is true for oil, which is an unpolar liquid, and water, which is a polar liquid. Corn syrup, on the other hand, has the ability to mix with water and thus can dissolve in it. This is what happens when you shake the jar really hard.

You can try many more objects and liquids to create even more layers; it is just a matter of density that will determine where they settle in your density column!

CLEANUP · · · · · · · · · · · · ·
You can pour all the liquids from the jars down the drain. Clean any spills.

How Heavy Is Your Air?

BALLOONS AWAY! YOU'VE SEEN A HELIUM BALLOON FLOAT, BUT WHAT GAS COULD MAKE A BALLOON HEAVIER THAN AIR? TRY THIS DENSE PHYSICS ACTIVITY, AND FIND OUT!

If you've ever accidentally let go of a helium-filled balloon while outdoors, then you know that some gases are less dense than others. In the case of your helium balloon, it most likely floated away before you could catch it because helium is much lighter (or less dense) than the air in our environment. We don't often think about gases having density—but they do! In this activity, you'll explore the different densities of some common household gases, including the air that you exhale!

PROJECT TIME
30 minutes

KEY CONCEPTS
Physics
Chemistry
Density
Gas

41

BACKGROUND ·····················

All of the materials we encounter on a daily basis, from our toothpaste to our dinner plates, are made up of different types of atoms. Atoms are the smallest units of matter that retain the properties of their chemical element. The type and arrangement of these different atoms account for the different characteristics of all the solids, liquids, and gases in our environment.

These characteristics include properties known as density, mass, and volume. The density of an object is the relationship between its mass (weight) and its volume (amount of space it takes up). The mass of an object's atoms, their size, and how they are arranged all determine its density. If we know an object's mass and volume, we can figure out the density using the equation: density = mass/volume.

From this equation, we can also observe that if two objects have the same volume but one weighs more than the other, than the two objects have different densities. If you have a die made from plastic and another die of the same size made from lead, the one made from lead will feel heavier. Because the two dice are the same size, we know the lead is denser than the plastic.

Differences in density have to do with the size of the atoms as well as how tightly they are packed together. The atoms that comprise metal are generally heavier than those of plastic and are packed more closely together. In this activity, you will be observing the density of different gases—and how differences in density affect how an object behaves.

MATERIALS ~~~~~~~~~~~~~~~

- Yardstick
- Two balloons
- 4 tablespoons baking soda
- Stopwatch or timer
- 1 cup (236 ml) white vinegar
- Clean 16-ounce (0.5 l) plastic water or soda bottle
- Small plastic funnel (If unavailable, use tinfoil or parchment paper to make a temporary funnel.)
- A partner to help
- A sink
- Pencil or pen
- Sheet of paper

PREPARATION

- Create a table on your sheet of paper with three columns and three rows.

- Label the left column: "Balloon." Write: "Balloon A" in the middle box and "Balloon B" in the bottom box. Label the middle column: "3-Foot (0.9 m) Drop"; label the right column: "6-Foot (1.8 m) Drop."

PROCEDURE

- Carefully pour the vinegar into the water bottle.

- Carefully pour the baking soda into one of the balloons using your funnel. Do not tie it closed. Hold it carefully so that the baking soda does not spill out.

- Secure the baking soda-filled balloon to the top of the water bottle. Avoid letting the baking soda fall into the bottle. To do this, hold the mouth of the balloon and shake the baking soda down to the bottom. Keep holding it this way while you gently cover the top of the bottle with the mouth of the balloon, not allowing the contents of the balloon to drop into the bottle.

- Ensure that the mouth of the balloon covers the bottle top as completely and securely as possible.

- Place the bottle in the sink. Note the size of the balloon and the appearance of the vinegar in the bottle.

- Carefully tip the balloon vertically so the baking soda spills into the bottle. *What happens when the baking soda comes into contact with the vinegar in the bottle? Is the liquid in the bottle changing? What happens to the balloon? What do you think is causing the balloon to change shape?*

- When the reaction slows, you can gently shake the bottle and tap the balloon, to ensure that no baking soda is stuck in the balloon or on the sides of the bottle.

43

- When the reaction is complete, ask your partner to help you remove the balloon from the bottle without allowing gas to escape the balloon. While the balloon is still attached, have your partner tightly squeeze the balloon closed just above where its mouth meets the bottle. With the balloon held closed, you can gently remove it from the bottle. (Don't be surprised if a puff of gas escapes from the bottle when you remove the balloon!)

- Tie off the balloon. This is "Balloon A."

- Take the second balloon and blow it up to the same size as Balloon A and tie it off. This second balloon is "Balloon B."

- Have your partner hold the yardstick vertically, resting the end on the floor. They should also hold your stopwatch or timer.

- Stand next to your partner and hold Balloon A at the top of the yardstick, so that it is exactly 3 feet (0.9 m) off the floor.

- Drop the balloon and at the same time have your partner start the timer.

- Note how long it takes the balloon to fall to the ground. Record this time in your table.

- Repeat the balloon-drop steps with Balloon B. *Which balloon took longer to drop to the ground?*

- Have your partner use the yardstick to measure 6 feet (1.8 m) from the ground. (It's easier if you do this against a wall.)

- Repeat the balloon-drop steps, dropping each balloon from 6 feet (1.8 m). Record your results in your table.

ExTRA

Test to see the maximum distance that you can throw each balloon. *Is one easier to throw than the other? Why do you think that is?*

OBSERVATIONS AND RESULTS ·········

In this activity, you created the gas carbon dioxide (CO_2) by combining baking soda and vinegar. Both are known as the reactants in this reaction because they undergo a change while taking part in the reaction. Vinegar is weakly acidic whereas baking soda is a bicarbonate. When they are combined, a two-step reaction takes place. The first step of the reaction is an acid-base reaction, and the second step is a decomposition reaction. When both steps are complete, the final products are CO_2 and water (H_2O). When you added the baking soda to the vinegar, you should have observed bubbling and foaming in the bottle. This was the CO_2 gas being produced and released. The reaction produced too much CO_2 for the bottle to hold, however. As a result, the CO_2 gas escaped into Balloon A and the balloon expanded. Once all of the baking soda mixed with the vinegar, the contents of the bottle were CO_2 and H_2O. When there was nothing left to react, the reaction ended.

Your next step in this activity was measuring the rate that the two different balloons dropped to the ground. As you know, Balloon A contained CO_2 from the baking soda and vinegar reaction. In contrast, Balloon B contained the air you exhaled while blowing it up. The air we exhale is mostly nitrogen and oxygen, and only about 4 to 5 percent carbon dioxide. Therefore, you were measuring whether the mostly pure carbon dioxide in Balloon A dropped more quickly than the mostly nitrogen and oxygen gas in Balloon B.

You should have found that Balloon A dropped more quickly to the ground than Balloon B. You probably noticed that Balloon B encountered greater air resistance on the way to the floor. Balloon B's path might not have been straight down, instead the balloon may have floated around as it fell. Because both balloons were the same size (or volume) but one fell more quickly than the other, our results tell us the CO_2 gas in Balloon A is denser than the combination of gases found in Balloon B.

CLEANUP ··························

Pop and throw away the balloons. Pour the vinegar and baking soda mixture into the sink and rinse the bottle for recycling. Return all other materials to where you found them.

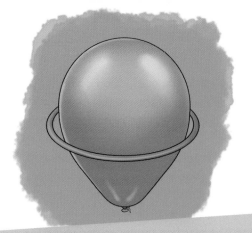

⚛ Size-Changing Science
How Gases Contract and Expand

FIND OUT MORE ABOUT THE CHARACTERISTICS OF GASES IN THIS CHEMISTRY CHALLENGE.

Have you ever baked—or purchased—a loaf of bread, muffins, or cupcakes and admired the fluffy final product? If so, you have appreciated the work of expanding gases! They are everywhere—from the kitchen to the cosmos. You've sampled their pleasures every time you've eaten a slice of bread, bitten into a cookie, or sipped a soda. In this science activity, you'll capture a gas in a stretchy container you're probably pretty familiar with—a balloon! This will let you to observe how gases expand and contract as the temperature changes.

PROJECT TIME
1 hour

KEY CONCEPTS
Chemistry
States of matter
Gases
Energy
Temperature

46

BACKGROUND ·····································

Everything in the world around you is made up of matter, including an inflated balloon and what's inside of it. Matter comes in four different forms, known as states, which go (generally) from lowest to highest energy. They are: solids, liquids, gases, and plasmas. Gases, such as the air or helium inside a balloon, take the shape of the containers they're in. They spread out so that the space is filled up evenly with gas molecules. The gas molecules are not connected. They move in a straight line until they bounce into another gas molecule or hit the container's wall, and then they rebound and continue in another direction until they hit something else. The combined motion energy of all of the gas molecules in a container is called the average kinetic energy.

This average kinetic (motional) energy changes in response to temperature. When gas molecules are warmed, their average kinetic energy also increases. This means they move faster and have more frequent and harder collisions inside of the balloon. When cooled, the kinetic energy of the gas molecules decreases, meaning they move more slowly and have less frequent and weaker collisions.

MATERIALS

- Freezer with some empty space
- Two latex balloons that will inflate to approximately 9 to 12 inches (23 to 30 cm)
- Piece of string, at least 20 inches long (51 cm)
- Permanent marker
- Cloth tape measure. (A regular tape measure or ruler can also work, but a cloth tape measure is preferable.)
- Scrap piece of paper and a pen or pencil
- Clock or timer
- A helper

PREPARATION ·····································

- Make sure your freezer has enough space to easily fit an inflated balloon inside. The balloon should not be smushed or squeezed at all. If you need to move food to make space, be sure to get permission from anybody who stores food in the freezer. Also make sure to avoid any pointy objects or parts of the freezer.

47

- Blow up a balloon until it is mostly—but not completely—full. Then carefully tie it off with a knot. With your helper assisting you, measure the circumference of the widest part of the balloon using a cloth tape measure or a piece of string (and then measure the string against a tape measure). *What is the balloon's circumference?*

- Inflate another balloon so it looks about the same size as the first balloon, but don't tie it off yet. Pinch the opening closed between your thumb and finger so the air cannot escape. Have your helper measure the circumference of the balloon, then adjust the amount of air inside until it is within about 1/2 inch (1.3 cm) or less (plus or minus) of the first balloon's circumference (by blowing in more air or letting a little escape). Then tie off the second balloon.

PROCEDURE

- Turn one of the balloons so you can look at the top of it. At the very top it should have a slightly darker spot. Using the permanent marker, carefully make a small spot in the center of the darker spot.

- Then take a cloth tape measure (or use a piece of string and a regular tape measure or ruler), and carefully make two small lines with the permanent marker at the top of the balloon that are 2 1/2 inches (6.3 cm) away from one another, with the darker spot as the midpoint. To do this, you can center the tape measure so that its 1 1/4-inch (3.1 cm) mark is on the small spot you made and then make a line at the 0 and 2 1/2-inch (6.3 cm) points.

- Repeat this with the other balloon so that it also has lines that are 2 1/2 inches (6.3 cm) apart on its top.

- Somewhere on one balloon write the number "1" and on the other balloon write the number "2."

- Because it can be difficult to draw exact lines on a balloon with a thick permanent marker, now measure the exact distance between the two lines you drew on each balloon, measuring from the outside of both lines. (For example, the distance might be 2 3/8 inches [6 cm] or 2 5/8 inches [6.6 cm].) Write this down for each balloon (with the balloon's number) on a scrap piece of paper. *Why do you think it's important to be so exact when measuring the distances?*

- Put balloon number 1 in the freezer in the area you cleared out for it. Leave it in the freezer for 45 minutes. Do not disturb it or open the freezer during this time. *How do you think the size of the balloon will change from being in the freezer?*

- During this time, leave balloon number 2 somewhere out at room temperature (not in direct sunlight or near a hot lamp).

- After balloon number 1 has been in the freezer for 45 minutes, bring your cloth tape measure (or piece of string and regular tape measure) to the freezer and, with the balloon still in the freezer (but with the freezer door open to let you access the balloon), quickly measure the distance between the two lines as you did before. *Did the distance between the two lines change? If so, how did it change? What does this tell you about whether the size of the balloon changed? Why do you think this is?*

- Then measure the distance between the two lines on balloon number 2, which stayed at room temperature. *Did the distance between the two lines change? If so, how did it change? How did the balloon's size change? Why do you think this is?*

- *Overall, how did the balloon change size when placed in the freezer? What do your results tell you about how gases expand and contract as temperature changes?*

EⅹTRA

After taking balloon number 1 out of the freezer leave it at room temperature for at least 45 minutes to let it warm up. Then remeasure the distance between the lines. *How has the balloon changed size after warming up, if it changed at all?*

⚛ SCIENCE FAIR IDEA

Try this activity again but instead of putting balloon number 1 in the freezer, put it in a hot place for 45 minutes, such as outdoors on a hot day or inside a car on a warm day. (Just make sure the balloon is not in direct sunlight or near a hot lamp, as this can deflate the balloon by letting the gas escape.) *Does the balloon change size when put in a hot place? If so, how?*

⚛ SCIENCE FAIR IDEA

In this activity, you used air from your lungs but other gases might behave differently. You could try this activity again but this time fill the balloons with helium. *How does using helium affect how the balloon changes size when placed in a freezer?*

OBSERVATIONS AND RESULTS • • • • • • • • • •

Did balloon number 1, which was placed in the freezer, shrink a little compared with balloon number 2, which stayed at room temperature?

You should have seen that when you put the balloon in the freezer, the distance between the lines decreased a little, from about 2 1/2 inches (6.3 cm) to 2 1/4 inches (5.7 cm) (or by 1/4 inch [0.6 cm], about 10 percent). The balloon shrank! The distance between the lines on the balloon kept at room temperature should have pretty much stayed the same (or decreased very slightly), meaning that the balloon shouldn't have really changed size. The frozen balloon shrank because the average kinetic energy of the gas molecules in a balloon decreases when the temperature decreases. This makes the molecules move more slowly and have less frequent and weaker collisions with the inside wall of the balloon, which causes the balloon to shrink a little. But if you let the frozen balloon warm up, you would find that it gets bigger again, as big as the balloon that you left at room temperature the whole time. This is because the average kinetic energy would increase due to the warmer temperature, making the molecules move faster and hit the inside of the balloon harder and more frequently again.

CLEANUP ·····························

Deflate and throw out your used balloons. Replace all other materials where you found them.

Suck It Up—with Cooling Air!

WHAT WARMS UP... SEE HOW YOU CAN MAKE LIQUID DEFY GRAVITY USING JUST TEMPERATURE DIFFERENCES!

You may know many objects expand (or get bigger) when they get hot and shrink when they cool down. For example, this is true for metals, wood, and concrete. But did you know that gases do the same? It is just difficult to see when it happens. This activity will let you "see" air contract using water!

PROJECT TIME
45 minutes

KEY CONCEPTS
Physics
Gases
Temperature
Expansion and contraction

BACKGROUND

Matter, such as a solid, liquid, or gas, is defined as "a substance that has mass and takes up space by having volume." If matter is heated, it has the tendency to change its shape, area and volume. This property is called thermal expansion. The reason this change happens is due to the fact that all matter is made up of atoms and molecules, which behave differently depending on whether they are hot or cold. When heated, molecules begin to vibrate and move around very fast. This leads to their greater separation, which results in the expansion of the material. When cooled, however, molecules tend to move much less, which makes them take up much less space.

Liquid thermometers are a great application of thermal expansion. The liquid, which is trapped in a little glass tube, changes its volume due to an increase or decrease in temperature. If it gets hotter, the liquid expands and rises in the glass tube, indicating higher temperature. If it gets colder, the liquid contracts and its level in the tube drops, indicating a lower temperature. The exact amount of volume change can then be correlated to the temperature change. This allows us to read the temperature from the liquid level inside the thermometer.

In this activity, you will also make liquid rise inside a glass—not due to thermal expansion of the liquid but due to thermal contraction of the gas above the liquid. Confused? Then do this activity and find out how it works!

MATERIALS

- Two identical flat plates
- Ice cubes
- Two identical, transparent drinking glasses
- A large bowl (It should be deep enough so one of the glasses can be submerged inside it.)
- Tap water (hot and cold)
- Food coloring (optional)

PREPARATION

- Carefully fill the bowl with hot tap water (the hottest setting that you have).

- Submerge one of the glasses in the water so that it is completely covered and filled by water.

- Keep the other glass at room temperature.

- Place the ice cubes on one of the flat plates and add cold water, so that the whole plate is covered with ice water.

- Pour some room temperature water on the second plate so that it is also covered with water.

- Optionally, you can add one or two drops of food coloring to the water on both of the plates to make the phenomenon more visible.

PROCEDURE •••••••••••••••••••••••••••••••

- Feel the temperature of the water on both plates with your finger. *Are the temperatures very different?*

- Carefully take the glass out of the bowl with hot water. *How does the glass feel? Is it very hot?*

- Push the ice cubes to the sides on the plate and place the glass upside down on the flat plate with the ice water. *What happens to the glass when you put it on the plate? What happens to the liquid on the plate?*

- Observe the glass for five to 10 minutes. *Does anything change with the liquid or the glass over that time period? If yes, what happens? Can you explain your observations?*

- After 10 minutes, remove the glass from the plate. *How does the glass feel this time? Did its temperature change during the test?*

- Next, take the second glass that was not submerged in the bowl and place it upside down on the second plate with room temperature water. *What do you think will happen to the water on the plate and the glass this time?*

- Again, observe the glass for five to 10 minutes. *Do you see any changes happening? Are the results the same as before? Whether you answer yes or no, can you explain why?*

ExTRA

Can you find out exactly how much water your glass can suck up? Add different amounts of water to the plate and test it! You might need to use a bigger plate if you want to add more water.

ExTRA

How much of a temperature difference between the glass and the water on the plate is required to suck the water up? Fill the bowl with warm water (instead of hot water) and repeat the test. You can also vary the temperature of the water on the plate. Does it need to be ice water? How big does the temperature difference need to be?

⚛ SCIENCE FAIR IDEA

Does changing your glass container to something bigger or smaller change your results? Does the shape of the glass matter? Design tests to find out!

OBSERVATIONS AND RESULTS ·········

When you put the warm glass onto the plate with cold water, you should have seen the water rise up inside the glass. The glass is initially heated when submerged in hot water. Once you take it out of the bowl, the water inside the glass is replaced by air, which then is warmed too. When you put the glass upside down onto the layer of ice water on the plate, the ice water cools down the glass and the warm air inside. This causes the air inside the glass to contract (its molecules do not bounce around as much).

The contracting air inside the glass exerts a lower pressure (the "push" air molecules exert on surfaces they are in contact with) on the water in the glass than the room-temperature air outside the glass. This causes water to be pushed up into the glass, compressing the air inside. Eventually the pressure difference balances out, and the rising water stops. In other words, the shrinking volume of the air inside the glass is replaced with water. This does not happen if the glass and the water on the plate are at the same temperature. The air inside the glass has no reason to cool down, so it remains at the same volume and pressure, and there is nothing to push water up into the glass.

CLEANUP ··············

Pour leftover water and ice into the sink. Dry your plates and glasses. Replace all materials to where you found them.

Chilling Science
Evaporative Cooling with Liquids

NOW THAT'S COOL! LEARN HOW TO COOL IT DOWN WITH EVAPORATION.

PROJECT TIME

15 minutes

KEY CONCEPTS

Physics
Evaporation
Heat transfer
Temperature

Have you ever wondered why we sweat when our environment is hot or when we exercise? Sweating is a life-saving strategy that cools the body down and maintains its temperature. Without sweating, the body cannot regulate its temperature, which can lead to overheating or even heatstroke. But why does sweating have a cooling effect? The answer is evaporative cooling. Turning a liquid such as sweat from its liquid state into a gas requires energy. This energy is taken from our body, or sweat, in the form of heat. The resulting heat transfer leads to the desired cooling effect. In this activity, you can observe this cooling power in action—ready to get cool?

57

BACKGROUND

The process of changing a liquid into its gaseous state is called evaporation. Every liquid can be turned into a gas if enough energy is added to the liquid in the form of heat. The energy needed for the transformation is known as the heat of evaporation. How much energy you need depends on factors such as the type of liquid or the surrounding temperature. If it is already very hot outside, you will need less energy to vaporize a liquid; if it is very cold, you will need more.

In order to turn into a gas, the molecules held together inside the liquid have to break free to get into the air. This means the hydrogen bonds holding the molecules together need to be broken. Thus, molecules that are able to form lots of hydrogen bonds among themselves are much harder to turn into a gas and have a higher heat of evaporation. This also affects the boiling temperature of a liquid. Molecules that attract one another very strongly start to boil at higher temperatures compared with those that have weak attractions. A lower boiling point generally means a liquid will evaporate more quickly. Water, for example, with one oxygen and two hydrogen atoms, can form two hydrogen bonds per molecule. Its heat of evaporation is 2,260 joules per gram, or 541 calories per gram, and it starts boiling at 212°F (100°C).

Your body makes use of the evaporative process when sweating. Sweat, which consists of 90 percent water, starts to evaporate. The necessary heat of evaporation is extracted from the sweat itself, which leads to a heat transfer from the liquid into the gaseous state. This results in a cooling effect (called evaporative cooling) that helps to maintain body temperature and cools the body down when it gets too hot. The degree of cooling is dependent on the evaporation rate and heat of evaporation. In this activity, you will find out which liquid has a greater cooling power: rubbing alcohol or water. What do you think will cool more when it evaporates?

MATERIALS

- Rubbing alcohol
- Water
- Two small cups or bowls
- Tablespoon
- Pipettete or medical dropper

PREPARATION

- Fill one small cup or bowl with 1 tablespoon (15 ml) of water.

- Fill the second small cup or bowl with 1 tablespoon (15 ml) of rubbing alcohol.

PROCEDURE

- Suck up some water from the first bowl (water) using the pipette or medical dropper.

- Carefully drop one or two drops on the back of your hand and spread the liquid with your fingers. *When the water touches your skin, how does it feel?*

- Blow softly over the skin area that you just covered with water. *Does your skin feel any different when blowing on the water? Can you sense a difference in temperature while blowing? How does it feel?*

- Rinse your pipette with some rubbing alcohol and then suck up some of the alcohol with your pipette.

- Drop the same quantity of liquid on the back of your other hand and spread the liquid with your fingers. *Does the alcohol feel different when it touches your skin? How?*

- Again, blow over the area on your hand where you put the alcohol. *What sensation do you feel? Does your hand feel warmer or cooler compared with water when blowing on the liquid? Can you think of a reason why?*

ExTRA

Find out how fast rubbing alcohol and water evaporate. Put the same (small) amount of water and rubbing alcohol in two different cups and place them both in the sun. Observe how long it takes for the liquids to completely evaporate. (Depending on how warm it is, this might take some time.) *Which liquid vaporizes faster?* You can even determine the evaporation rate by weighing the cups in the beginning and throughout your experiment to find out how much water is lost due to evaporation.

OBSERVATIONS AND RESULTS · · · · · · · · ·

Did you feel the cooling power of water and rubbing alcohol? Both liquids should feel cold on your skin. Blowing on your wet hand helps the water and alcohol to evaporate. The airflow will also support the heat transfer away from your skin. You should have noticed that your skin feels much cooler when you put the rubbing alcohol on your hand compared with the water. The water and the alcohol will start to evaporate once you start blowing on your hand. Compared with water, alcohol has a lower heat of evaporation. That means that for the same amount of liquid, more heat transfer occurs during the evaporation of water compared with the alcohol.

This does not fit your observation that alcohol has a greater cooling effect than water, however. The reason for that is that the amount of heat transfer also depends on the evaporation rate. As alcohol evaporates at a much faster rate compared with water due to its lower boiling temperature of 180°F (82°C) (compared to 212°F [100°C]), it is able to carry away more heat from the skin. This means, for a given amount of time, much more alcohol evaporates than water. You probably noticed this also if you did the extra activity of putting the same amount of alcohol and water outside in the sun and monitored their evaporation rates. Other factors that influence evaporation rates are the surface area, temperature and airflow.

CLEANUP ·

Flush any unused rubbing alcohol down the sink with plenty of cold water. Wash your hands with soap, and clean your work area.

THE SCIENTIFIC METHOD

The scientific method helps scientists—and students—gather facts to prove whether an idea is true. Using this method, scientists come up with ideas and then test those ideas by observing facts and drawing conclusions. You can use the scientific method to develop and test your own ideas!

Question: What do you want to learn? What problem needs to be solved? Be as specific as possible.

Research: Learn more about your topic and refine your question.

Hypothesis: Form an educated guess about what you think will answer your question. This allows you to make a prediction you can test.

Experiment: Create a test to learn if your hypothesis is correct. Limit the number of variables, or elements of the experiment that could change.

Analysis: Record your observations about the progress and results of your experiment. Then analyze your data to understand what it means.

Conclusion: Review all your data. Did the results of the experiment match the prediction? If so, your hypothesis was correct. If not, your hypothesis may need to be changed.

GLOSSARY

bond: The force that holds atoms or molecules together.

circumference: The length around the widest part of a sphere.

control: A group not treated with something that is being tested in an experiment to allow for comparison with a group that has been treated with something.

correlate: To have a close correlation, or a relationship in which things happen and change together.

density: The amount of a matter in a given area or material.

intermittently: The state of not happening steadily, or stopping and starting and stopping again.

irritate: To make sore, painful, or uncomfortable.

lattice: A structure of that looks like crossed strips.

miscibility: The ability of two substances to mix together completely regardless of amount.

particle: A very small piece.

predict: To guess what will happen in the future based on facts or knowledge.

reaction: A response when two or more chemicals are mixed together.

regulate: To adjust the rate or amount of something.

solute: The substance being dissolved in a liquid.

solvent: The liquid used to dissolve another substance.

thermal: Having to do with heat.

viscous: Thick or sticky and unable to flow easily.